# Animals
## Day and Night

By Katharine Kenah

WATERBIRD BOOKS
Columbus, Ohio

Library of Congress Cataloging-in-Publication Data

Kenah, Katharine.
    Animals day and night/by Katharine Kenah.
            p.cm.--(Extreme readers. Beginning one reader)
    ISBN 0-7696-3183-5 (pbk.)
    1. Nocturnal animals--Juvenile literature. I. Title. II. Series.

QL755.K465 2004
591.5'18--dc22

                                            2004040254

Copyright © 2004 School Specialty Children's Publishing.  Published by Waterbird Books,
an imprint of School Specialty Children's Publishing, a member of the School Specialty
Family.

Send all inquiries to:
School Specialty Children's Publishing
8720 Orion Place
Columbus, OH 43240-2111


ISBN 0-7696-3183-5

4 5 6 7 8 9 10 11 PHXBK 10 09 08 07 06 05 04

Day is over.
The sun goes down.
Many animals
go to sleep.
But some animals
wake up.

# Koala

By day, a koala
sleeps in a tree.
At night, it eats
tree leaves.

# Hippopotamus

By day, a hippopotamus sleeps in the water.
At night, it eats plants.

# Opossum

By day, an opossum swings from a tree. At night, it looks for food to eat.

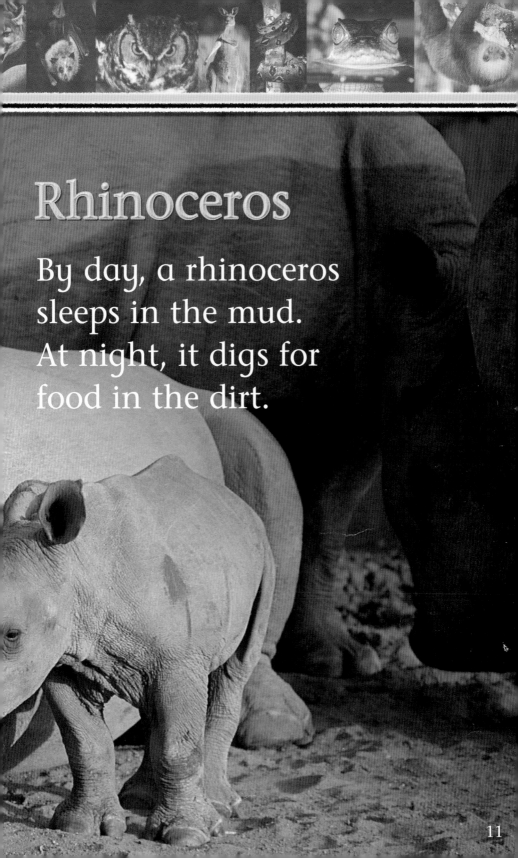

# Rhinoceros

By day, a rhinoceros sleeps in the mud. At night, it digs for food in the dirt.

# Skunk

By day, a skunk sleeps in a hole. At night, it looks for food to eat.

# Sun Bear

By day, a sun bear
sleeps in the sun.
At night, it eats
bugs and honey.

# Green Turtle

By day, a green turtle
swims in the water.
At night, it lays eggs
on the beach.

# Cougar

By day, a cougar
sleeps in the hills.
At night, it looks
for animals to eat.

# Fruit Bat

By day, a fruit bat
hangs from a tree.
At night, it eats fruit.

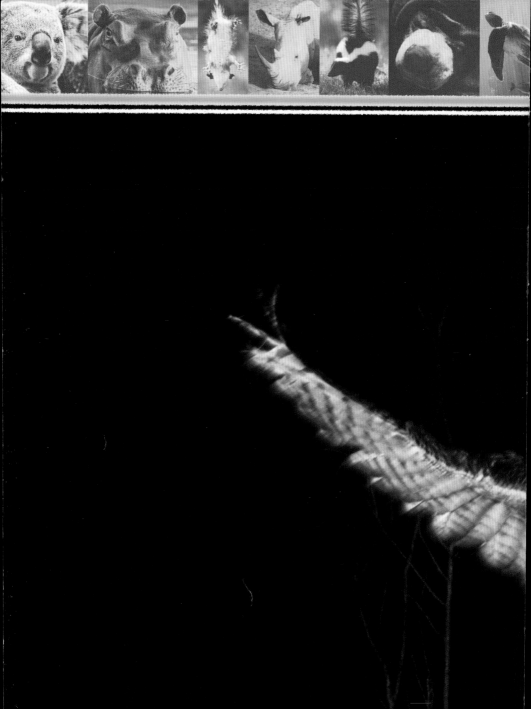

# Owl

By day, an owl
sits in a tree.
At night, it looks
for mice to eat.

# Kangaroo

By day, a kangaroo
sleeps in a cool place.
At night, it eats
small plants.

# Boa Constrictor

By day, a boa constrictor
sleeps in a tree.
At night, it eats its
food whole!

# Caiman

By day, a caiman
stays in the water.
At night, it looks
for food to eat.

# Two-Toed Sloth

By day, a sloth
sleeps in a tree.
At night, it eats
fruit and leaves.

# EXTREME FACTS ABOUT ANIMALS DAY AND NIGHT!

- Koalas rarely drink water! They get the water they need from eating tree leaves.

- On land, hippos can run as fast as human beings.

- When opossums sense danger, they pretend to faint and play dead.

- Rhinos can live almost 50 years.

- Skunks can spray things 12 feet away!

- Sun bears are about the size of large dogs.

- Female green turtles may swim thousands of miles to lay eggs on the beach where they were born.

- Cries of wild cougars are very startling. They sound like women screaming.

- So many fruit bats will hang in one tree that it looks like the tree is loaded with fruit.

- Owls see mostly in black and white.

- Baby kangaroos are only an inch long when they are born.

- The bones of boa constrictors' jaws stretch apart so they can swallow prey much larger than their heads.

- Caimans have 72-78 long, sharp teeth, but they swallow their prey whole!

- Sloths give birth upside down in trees.